THE CITY, OUR CITY

ALSO BY WAYNE MILLER

POETRY COLLECTIONS

The Book of Props

Only the Senses Sleep

CHAPBOOKS

O City

What Night Says to the Empty Boat (Notes for a Film in Verse)

TRANSLATIONS

I Don't Believe in Ghosts, by Moikom Zeqo

EDITED BOOKS

Tamura Ryuichi: On the Life & Works of a 20th Century Master
 (with Takako Lento)

New European Poets (with Kevin Prufer)

THE CITY, OUR CITY

WAYNE MILLER

MILKWEED EDITIONS

Published 2011 by Milkweed Editions
Printed in Canada
Cover and interior design by Gretchen Achilles/Wavetrap Design
Cover photo by Abelardo Morell
Author photo by Jeanne Ouellette
The text of this book is set in Minion Pro.

11   12   13   14   15   5   4   3   2   1

FIRST EDITION

Please turn to the back of this book for a list of the sustaining funders of Milkweed
Editions.

Library of Congress Cataloging-in-Publication Data

Miller, Wayne, 1976–
    The city, our city / Wayne Miller. -- 1st ed.
        p. cm.
    Includes bibliographical references.
    ISBN 978-1-57131-445-1 (pbk. : acid-free paper) -- ISBN 978-1-57131-830-5 (e-Book)
    I. Title.
    PS3613.I56245C58 2011
    811'.6--dc22

                                                                2010033724

This book is printed on acid-free paper.

This book is for my parents, who first took me to the City

and for Harper Elyse, who will inherit it

CONTENTS

. . . they pushed on, raised the flag of the Word
Upon lawless spots denied or forgotten
By the fear or the pride of the Glittering City . . .

—W. H. AUDEN

the city that wakes every hundred years and looks
    at itself in the mirror of a word and doesn't
    recognize itself and goes back to sleep . . .

—OCTAVIO PAZ

Thus the city repeats its life, identical, shifting up
and down on its empty chessboard.

—ITALO CALVINO

THE CITY, OUR CITY

A PRAYER (O CITY—)

O arrow landed deep in Harold's eye—

O voice
          pressing upward against the sky—

O light and steam.

(When the western windows
of the City go pink, the rooms behind them
lock shut with clouds.)

O clouds—

          (Slipping down in the morning
to part around the skyrises, to marble
the rooftop shanties and gardens,
the hammocks and clotheslines.)

And graying water tanks—

                    (Our water lifted
into the clouds—and me, drawing it
down into my cup, my breath
pressed to the shimmering surface.)

O City—
          (That breathes itself
into the glass—that pulls me to the window
I press my gaze through,
I press my face to—)

O City—

      (And the makers,
who drew the City through the membranes
of paper and canvas,
giving the city to the City—)

                       O City—

(And our tables and demitasses,
woofers and fire escapes,
kisses in doorways, weapons
and sculptures, concerts
and fistfights, sex toys and votives,
engines and metaphors—.)

City of Joists—

(The City shot through with them.)

City of Doorways—
                   (The City opens us,
and we step through.)

O Light-Coming-on-in-a-Window—

(Since you've opened the fridge,
opened your book, opened your room
to the room next door.)

O City—
   (Pushing through the dark
like the nose of a plane.)

O City—
   (It could be a bomber,
night-black, the instruments on auto,
the pilot asleep in his lounger.)

O City—
   (In the hull below, words
are written on the bombs in Sharpie.)

———

(There's also a folder of letters lying off to the side in the dark.

In one of them, the pilot's brother describes some fingerprints he's found pressed inside the lip of a broken jar.

He's an archeologist. The prints are from the jar's maker—just after the Battle of Hastings, near the end of the eleventh century.)

I

When a drop of water was found
floating on the sand, they dug a well;

and soon streets opened outward
from the core like petals, and voices

came together into houses full of air.
Houses of mudbrick and straw

clustered beneath the ridgeline
like the pieces of a dropped jar. Until

design imposed its will, and men
of power ordered the new streets

carved at right angles—across
the natural topography—and soon

building was a profession, and builders
wore the products of tailors

living in what the builders had made.
Then the City grew beautiful—

its nutlike center surrounded
by boulevards and blocks and blocks

of rooms, and the top-floor windows
were beacons to distant travelers—

Take me to the bricks of light,
they cried, *those walls of backlit crosses.*

DEAR AUDEN,

The City in its ball rolled forward—

(the same City that, in its jar,
had engulfed the hill).

———

The City was the wall I lay on,

· then the City
was the voice I spoke into.

———

When gunmen exchanged fire

across my yard, the City
filled the bullets, which so briefly

breathed in their motion.

———

Later, the City was silence
threading through birdsongs.

———

I listened from the sun porch,

which seemed to hang
above the rotting picnic table.

———

The City was looped in the ring

I gave my lover to say: we would
live together inside the City.

———

Each July, the City hissed with light
at the sparklers' blinding cores.

———

When the City spread its darkness

over me, I loved the warmth
of the susurrations, and when the City

lifted me above the City

I leaned my head
against the egg-shaped window.

———

O Auden—O City—

what abstractions I had:
the illusions I swung from

along your neoned, crisscrossing,
paperflecked streets

———

I once believed
formed a bower of iron.

THE FEAST

1.

The table at which we sat had been destroyed in the war, then rebuilt from its pieces recovered behind the glassworks.

The food was sumptuous. Beyond the leaded windows there were hedgerows budding in lilac and white. When a streetcar passed clanging, I suppressed a sudden urge to ting my glass with my spoon.

Being strangers, we had little to talk about. So when at last Adam stood, we tipped forward into the words of his toast with the zeal that only strong liquor imparts.

From then on, things were better. We began to laugh. By eleven, I thought the night was a real success.

2.

I was lying just then—in truth we were terrified. We watched ourselves twist in the bells of our water glasses. How could we know who might stand to speak next, or what things he might say?

None of the servers could talk in our language. When an airplane buzzed the street, we all flinched in unison.

In the hills, there were distant bursts of artillery—then vast swatches of silence.

II

In the churches, stained glass
pressed blue upon the altars, priests

possessed the power of the bread
they held aloft. Nobles' weapons

were blessed, and the dark wine
the people drank filled them of course

with God. In a back-room ossuary
of monk-skull bricks, pilgrims

kissed a stranger's femur. What
can one say of such rooms?—bodies

turned inside out, flesh reduced
to stale pink wafers? Yet, the spire

of the Royal Cathedral kept
growing in its primitive scaffold,

workers all day mortaring
buttresses, carving eyes right into

the heads of statues—. And when
the scaffold was pulled away

the intricate tower hatched
into a world it already inhabited.

FLOODING THE VALLEY

Then the City rose in the valley,
filling first the long furrows
in thin glassy lines, then
the roads, the pastures, rising

up through the porch boards,
the floorboards, lifting bales
of hay from the fields, climbing
the fence posts, the woodpile,

rising in the sooted chimney
stone by stone, up the staircase
to slide across the wood floor,
soaking the featherbed,

past the top of the banister,
the grayed vanity mirror,
climbing the trunks of trees
until the leaves were swallowed,

the City then scaling the long
sides of the valley, dilating
as it rose toward the sky,
up its own great wall, where

cars lined the roadway,
where hands lined the railing—
then down the long chutes
in white braids of froth,

the City spilled out.

STREET FIGHT

What it was that filled me,
                                    filled me entirely.
The only space left
                        was inside my fists.

They came alive with me, as a window
comes alive with a sudden,
                                    human shape.

And I hurled myself against that fucker
who before
                    was my friend, who again

is my friend. Above us
                                the overpass
seethed with the arriving breakers

of tires, and when a car
                                rolled past
it honked and cheered us on. And when

I fell, the pavement confettied
                                    my palms,
and I slipped from my hands

so they became useless. Our shouting
shuttled between us

like a piston. And then
                    we were parched;
I found our bottle where I'd left it

by the mailbox,
                    and that was the end of it.
Except this lip, this knuckle.
                              —And you,

who watched from the windowdark,
dialtone
          pressed to your ear. Which

of our words spilled into the pillow
beside you? What
                    crisscross of circles

lapped at your sleep?

First: a face—and the light that hits it from the inside.

And someone notices that light and wants to keep it.

Soon: a color-slicked finger, then a brush,

then the void of a canvas—on which a room begins to appear.

And it goes without saying: there's all this time while the painter works—

the fan's blur in the window, the plastic rustling of ferns.

This goes on for days. Only once does he admit

a vague love for his subject sitting there—

shaping her face with his brush has a certain erotic appeal—

though soon he decides such love is merely a love for the work itself.

Sometimes they break for fruit and beer,

then almost too soon it's back to the work at hand.

So when a gunshot taps at the room's thin window,

they hardly notice, and when the war slides in like a storm cloud—

swallowing her up in its passing—he feels as if the damage done is not to the City or to them, finally, but to the painting.

Then reconstruction is finished; a friend gives him a camera—

and how he loves the idea of light striking the pictures into being.

He begins to photograph the façades and alleys,

the kiosks and cafés. Now the unfinished portrait haunts him;

he brings it up from the cellar. And the photograph he takes of it

at first is more to preserve his thoughts of those afternoons with her.

But then the portrait floating in the fixer's orange glow

emerges into a sealed and beautiful distance.

He blows it up and mounts it on fiberboard—and now

in that enlargement, more clearly than ever,

the image remains unfinished. He sets up the print on an easel,

takes out his oils and brushes, and begins to paint—

III

] and all wes then cleare, some faces
hath shadowes in them. Mister Preacher

marke the doores with crosses,
and ere long there is no winde in me

to stand on. Blesse us Lorde
with soupe and wine, bread and water

till we dye. And blesse Katheryn
with her long thin handes. You I saw

sucking the wordes from her mouth,
the light from her skin [

A HISTORY OF WAR

The fields buckled into earthworks,
breastworks, and the men dug deeper
into their ground. Of course, once
the trenches were cut, they could not

be moved—so the men adorned
the bunkers with card tables, slicked
the walls with posters, poured rum
into mugs they'd brought in from town.

Each morning, they stood-to, glared
down their rifles, through the nets
of barbed wire, the craters and corpses,
the litter of branches, footprints

and shells. Across the way, bayonets
just like theirs aimed back, as if
the parados propped mirrors, as if
their own blackened faces were hard

set against them. Over there, just
as here, the color guard raised the flag,
the captains sloganeered through
their bullhorns. Everyone could hear

the echoing, and everyone roared
and shouted—because such words
were the river that carried them deeper,
that kept them from sinking.

Then, as was the ritual, at nine,
the men climbed down from the firestep,
shot craps on the duckboards, read
treatises in the dugouts on passion

and Passchendaele. Anything to kill
the time between assaults, to black out
the instants of losing. And lose
they did, the escadrilles circling over,

those night-cries from the fence
blotted slowly by death. Valor
just the mask they wore—something
to warm their faces when sleet

pricked the gas clouds, when
friends burst like wineskins, when
three days' rain turned their fingers
all spongy and white. Meanwhile

in the fortresses, behind the glacis,
the casemates were full of generals,
tapestries, old statues of justice
with her balancing scales: each pan

a trench—each trench full of men
peering through periscopes. So
when journalists reported napalm
at the front, the producers

changed the name to Mark 77,
and when the food supply ran out,
the leaders filled the news
pushing barrows of turkey and ham.

And the folks at home cheered, said
look at our wealth, said *we will surely
carry the day*. Still, in the trenches,
the men boiled leather for nourishment,

learned to eat rats—the same rats
that had eaten their fallen. Then:
our side won on the widescreen TV,
and the leaders took shots and cigars.

And when the last man officially
was killed, they changed the channel.
Yet, on the field, our now-protagonist
crossed the no-man's-land, waded

into the enemy's trench. There,
among the bunkers and dugouts,
he gathered posters, CDs, pins,
dictionaries, vacation brochures—.

And from the rucksack of a body
half-sunk in the mud, he pulled
a blueprint for a summerhouse.
At first, he wasn't sure—it wasn't

a typical spoil of war—but then
he imagined the house on his empty
plot of land—. As he considered
his life in this stranger's rooms

he sensed what felt like fear.
But focusing on the skylights
and foreign details, he could see
he was glad the man had been killed.

IDENTIFYING THE BODY

At first, I pictured his thoughts
resting in there—like coals,

which properly blown on
could be brought back to fire.

Against the doctor's directions
I touched his cheek; then

I knew the body was useless.
Every side of him was forever

turned inwardly away. I knelt
by the cold gurney—his last

cigarettes had filled his clothes
with smoke. That smell

was as close as I could come
to hearing him speak.

IV

Then trees were leveled and bound
into ships—spores on the night's

black water. Their lights carried
the City with them, their songs

held rooms inside them. One captain
watched his crew and thought

My children—; another cast them out
into the sea. Each morning,

when the sun raised the sails,
the cook served hardtack and raisins;

and when the wind collapsed,
the men raised the sails of cards.

Never mind the dying—constant
and everywhere. Each time

they landed, the City
landed with them; each thing

they saw they smuggled home
in their voices—e.g., the splintered

quarterdeck, the jellyfish blousing
the waves, the dusky palmlight

into which they wore their terror,
the tattooed faces of natives

they captured, who served them
chicory broth from behind

velvet curtains—and all such things
were bricked onto the City.

I'VE HEARD THAT OUTSIDE THE CITY

they peel back the fields with a lip of fire.

Their churches are made of rotted logs
and the false garments of their rituals.

Those people wear superstitions like worksuits.
Their sacred books

are meant to be handled, not understood.

Driving out there, you'll notice the road names
are mostly semi-literate description:

Rumblepatch Lane, Shoat Gutter Road,
Farm-to-Market, Route JJ—.

Notice the wandering cows,
the thick voices of grackles.

Watch the trees curl right over your car.

Heard the high warbling of their fiddles?—
like human cries stretched into sinew.

Art for them is a blister.

They're not like us,
their preachers shout in fervorous throes.

They know how to skin possums,
when not to take shelter
in those red, tipping barns.

They rev the engines of their pickups
in courtship.

They must be saved, *our preachers*
bellow through the barrels of microphones,

and we imagine reading to them
our novels, playing for them

our finely wrought tunes.

Through our telescopes, we can see
how they ride their mysterious,

bladed machines, push their strollers
through the gravel by the highway.

They die on the seats of their privies,
drunk in the whitefrosted fields.

When it's night out there,
the cupped light of a house, or a bar,

is the light of the entire world.

THE DEATH OF THE FRONTIER

It is during sleep that the distinction between good men
and bad is least apparent.

—ARISTOTLE

In the dream, we wandered farther

into our thoughts,
toward the waters at their edge,
the overhanging cliffs—

we forded rivers, sometimes

snow fell on the squat cactuses,
the taut canvas covers;
it slipped through the steam

bursting from the horses' nostrils.

When our wheels broke,
we balanced on the thumbs
of our footprints,

dragged the children behind us

on palettes we'd gathered
from the City's back alleys.
We attended to our huddling

voices, dark around the fire,

we tipped our heads back
to examine the stars, though
at that remove our words failed

to describe them. Their whispers

floated over us,
behind us, wrapped the horizon
we kept pushing toward.

When the thread of the idea

we tugged on as a guide
led us through the emberlit camps
of strangers,

we stabbed them in their sleep;

and when we circled the wagons
in the night, we made
of ourselves a city—

like an animal bristling its fur.

Then, slowly, we awoke:
we were back in our beds,
the lights of the City

in the windows, the bridge—

an idea threading the bay.
At breakfast we sat quietly
for a long time, the paper

open before us, its letters

winding down the page.
Now where would we go,
what should be next? The day

was crisp, the light, polleny—

and up the street, that film
we'd wanted to see for years
was still showing.

WINTER PASTORAL

Not enough snow to cover the landscape,

just enough to hover beneath it—
the far hills etched into paper,

the City floating upward
through the falling. Across the avenue

a light comes on, its room
a space the mind breathes into,

while here, snow
brushes the cold window,

the night slipping steadily past.

The sound of the wind—but the wind
has no sound, we hear

only the vibrations
of whatever it touches. How silent

this room would be
without the creaking trees, the flutelike

eaves, the poorly fitted sash stiles.
Love,
          when I kiss your sleeping body,

it's like one flake landing
in a snowfield: brief contact—

which becomes part of the field.

V

This bodie is nothing but detailes,
the doctor wrote, having found it

in a field and dragged it home,
spent his nights bent over it

with mirrored candles
peering into the pried-open eyes—

even there, the body was surface.
Yet, he was convinced it must

be filled with something other
than body, as a ball thrown

through the air is filled
with something other than ball,

and since the body had swallowed
the storm of the soul—

and since the body was his.

THE ASSASSINATION LECTURE

Here's the moment that killed him:
bullet piercing his temple, head
thrown back as if in deep laughter.

And here's us: the crowd lining
the street, waving our little flags,
which were stiff with dye. (A century ago,

we'd be pinkish dots of paint;
now we're these clusters of pixels.)
I can tell you (because I was there)

that our gazes were just cilia
stroking the car, our bodies
mere buoys marking a channel.

Here's the muzzleflash: a leaf
catching light. Here's a scream:
some pixels darkening. And class,

if you're to understand anything
of history, you have to see
it was the *moment* that killed him,

not the squeeze of the trigger,
not the network of phonecalls
that obtained the gun. Not those

in the government whose voices
threaded the lines, not the lover
whose complicity was suspect.

Not the killer's dear teacher,
who published those tracts
against the system in the journals

of the time. Look at the scene:
like a queen's slip showing,
though she wears one every day.

And now, students, in my pocket,
I have something special: the bullet,
which, as you've probably heard,

was stolen from the hospital, then
slipped quietly through the populace—
until it came to rest with me.

I'm going to pass it around.
Note its weight in your hand, even
look for a trace of blood. Here,

in our moment, this bullet's just
an inert little snout. It will start
in the front, then weave toward the back.

—Which of you is going to steal it?

THE BEAUTIFUL CITY (IN 32 STROKES)

(1) The neighborhood shop windows,
   with their shifting interiors of music and color—

(2) then the dusklight that sheets them with *now*.

———

(3) The same thing in language;
   for example: *a green orange*—.

———

(4) Shadows of winter
   branches stamped through the blinds,

(5) and then the last remaining leaf begins to ring.

———

(6) On the boardwalk in November, my lover's body
   was the warmest thing I could hold against me.

(7) We warmed each other: a closed circuit.

———

(8) What Caravaggio knew: the body's bright flash—

   before it disappears.

(9) Imagine the archeologist's surprise: the reliquary
    held nothing but pigment—

(10) living blue. Powdered lapis.

——

(11) And when the first few raindrops lifted the dust,

(12) the rain arrived to press it back down.

——

(13) So let's shift the scales through their modes—

(14) or else watch a single chord
    drag behind it the shadow of its minor equivalent.

——

(15) Would this silver ring still be pretty
    if it was found in a mass grave from last year's war?

(16) From an ancient one?

——

(17) And when the radio announced the invasion
     wasn't coming.

———

(18) When I held her narrow thigh beneath my hand.

———

(19) When the car alarm died,
     there was silence—

             (20) then crickets, surfacing—.

———

(21) Now the busboys in the lot cup their joint as they pass it;
     keeping it alive,
                 they diminish it:

(22) a pinlight, breathing.

———

(23) Impossible to hold a grace note
     if it's to remain a grace note—

(24) so in music we have the best descriptor
     of a living, human face.

———

(25) The singer sang at her vanity
only for herself

(26) though we were listening in the courtyard.

———

(27) How fog rings the streetlights in auras of breath;

(28) how dirty windows do the same thing.

———

(29) A hammer shaped this bell

(30) and thus the ring of every future note.

———

(31) Each glance, pressed into the world—

———

(32) then the world presses back:

a closed circuit.

IN THE MUSEUM: A PASTORAL

A student has set up a canvas
before Rubens' *Autumn Landscape*
to copy it. His wrist hovers
in the air before him

like a whole note, the brush
flitting outward from his mind;
the tiny bundle of lashes
at its tip leaves an echo of form.

Then it's back to the palette
for the next timbre of light,
the next pale fold of the fields,
which the trees will erase

when they, too, eventually
arrive. He begins to feel
as though he's the instrument
cutting a key. The crowds

pool briefly around him,
then drift on to the next
bank of rooms—as, later,
he'll slip through the streets,

past the silhouetted cafés,
toward his kitchen. The City
nothing but shirtsleeves,
the field sliding among them;

now and then it leaves
a whiff of yellow on a cuff.

VI

In the fields outside the City,
the City's cotton floated among sticks

and brambles, razorcup bolls,
redbrown soil cracked there beneath.

Hovered: phantasmic, white
thumbprints across the valley, the City

a daub of light beyond the river. Then
all that white, diffuse and buoyant,

collapsed from the fields, as if
overnight it found its weight and fell—

and coalesced into luminous piles:
bales stacked on palettes, loaded

on barges to be thinned on the City's
water-frames, spun into threads.

Said the City: forget the hands
that gathered this, the canvas sacks

that held it. Said the City: it was spun
from its fibers on machines,

into cloth that wrapped the City's
wandering bodies, which walked

the streets like mummies—the fields,
the bolls, all that radiant

weightlessness just the ghost they wore,
the ghost of process and time.

AMERICAN AUBADE

"The ship! The hearse!—the second hearse!" cried Ahab
from the boat; "its wood could only be American!"
                                              —HERMAN MELVILLE

This *now* when the light turns
the white fence blue,

———

                somewhere

a man steps triumphantly
forward into his life—

and ruins it. It will take him
twenty-two years

to discover this. What now?
Days become words

and like words
lose their carbon. Smoke

———

rises from the chimneys,
then the air conditioners whirr

against the descended
heat. While all around us,

folks keep lying down
inside their parents' fears—

and what of it? This is
what they *want*. See the girl

snapping a passerby
with her cell phone?

———

He was so ugly, she whispers
into the mouthpiece,

I just had *to show you*. Now
what should we say

when she asks us
the way to the Public Library?

———

See the prairie
full of coneflowers, timothy,

braided highways.
See the blue window-eye

of the Armenian church—
framed at the end

of the arcade of porches.
See the neighbors

cutting through? How many
one day will wake

to find they've lost
their voice? How many

won't need it back—
will have nothing

with which to fill it?
Time to scatter sawdust

———

onto that waxy pool
of blood in the back lot

of the West-O Apartments.
Bad enough to be locked out

of your house, but then
Em got her leg stuck

through the window, and then
the phone began to ring.

(When the crusaders
are finally captured

in our cycling footage,
who'll be able to say

if their hands are raised
in Praise or surrender?)

———

When the light releases
the fence into its white,

the portside window
is pinkfilled; and when

the *panadería* has flipped
its sign to open, still

Murphy's Gas is closed—
so the little boy keeps

jumping on the hose
to ring the bell. Look how

proud his mother is;
you can see it all the way

from here—in how
she scolds him. Once,

———

when I awoke inside
a bender of a night, I found

I'd been asleep (how long?)
on my building's rooftop

frontage wall. A siren
swept the street, and so

that wrongside step
I didn't take now sculpts

these letters' curves.
When the light is done

———

climbing the octaves
of color, I find I'm floating

in this loose transparency.
Look at the leaves

———

still pinched into buds,
the migrating crows

staining the yard with black
then lifting all at once

like the pieces of a mobile.
In the narrow gaps

between fenceboards,
neighbors are merely

shifting lines of color.
See the doughnut of sky

in that cracked CD
lying between the cars?

———

And as for the cat we found
mewing in the street,

his back half crushed—
odds are he was put to sleep.

Still, the whole ride
to the vet, you held him

flopping and bloody
in your arms,

and he was purring—

AMERICAN NOCTURNE

It doesn't exist, America. It's a name
you give to an abstract idea. . . .
—HENRY MILLER

1. Here in the Eye of the City,

the window of a passing car
pulls my reflection from the ether
for just an instant then slips it
back beneath the street,

while in all directions the City's
an intricate weave of light—
cupped poses and atoposes—,
while out in the fields

cows sleep among the blind
pumpjacks weightlessly bowing.
Now a trash bag of bottles
tossed into the alley dumpster

sounds like a dropped chandelier,
and when the back door
· of the Eastsider swings open
the notes from the Telecaster

playing inside are rounded,
like the fingertips that press them
into *here*—our modern alchemy:
a fingertap floods the room,

a whispered word spreads
like oil on the lot's black lake.
The washateria's exhaust fan
keeps spinning—each

angled blade chasing the next—
while across the street
my neighbor in his work clothes
sleeps on the couch, TV

blowing against his face.
I imagine the stained glass
of a brainscan in a dim hospital
room—thoughts shifting

like sand—could be the system
coming in off the coast
tonight, as I sit on my stoop
getting a little drunk—;

which is to say: a line out of focus
has lost its density; which is
to say: a drop of dye
spreading in a glass of water—

2. To Sleep in the City,

when the earth has closed
its eyelid across us, when the dark
is the wind fuzzing over
a microphone. We pinch ourselves

closed like lilies, dig into the sand
where the syllables lie,—
those knuckles, those vertebrae.
We must forget the body

lying in the dumpster, newspapers
covering it more deeply
each day. We must forget the City,
though we lift it together,

as in the blanket toss we learned
from the natives, just before
the City erased them. And while
the narratives of power

roll their ink across the continents,
roiling the air up into the next
historical map, I must
lie inside my body

and assure myself that everything
I've gathered will remain
just as I left it—such is the City's
promise. I'll forget the planes

passing overhead—dim ballpoints
of light—; I'll forget the wind
turning the pages of the book
I left open on the table—

VII

Down the quay, a mob
cornered a moor, dragged him

onto the bridge, roped his neck
and tossed him over. His body

hung for several days, until
an oarsman on a passing boat

knocked him into the water. Then
he was hanged again, and hanged

repeatedly for hundreds of years.
At night, when the cops passed

twirling their clubs, when the bars
sang their pressed-tin songs, folks

could see him from their windows,
his heavy corpse swaying

in the river breeze. Some enjoyed
the comfort of the ritual—

the body arriving like church
or fish at the end of the week—

while others felt sickened.
Yet, even on moonless nights

when the City was at its darkest,
no one wanted to be caught

sneaking onto the bridge
with a knife to cut the body down.

THE DEAD MOOR SPEAKS

The throngs slowed down to look at me.

The boys stood still, filling with world.

And I was the world they filled with, swinging

like the pendulum driving a clock,

like the empty noose before I filled it.

———

The men that night were opaque as—.

The water below me
never stopped moving. When a fly

landed on my tongue, I tried to shoo it
with my voice
                but I had no voice.

———

The boys were pointing
                at their world.
I swung before them like meat,

like the vote, like an openmouthed bucket
plumbing a well. One drop

held in mid-fall
above that river—*the City's dear river*—

———

and when a boatman passed, knocking me
into the water, its clarity remained.

SILENCE IN THE CITY

fills the bricks and the mortar between the bricks

the sheets of glass   the I-beams the City is riveted into

wells up in the streets to flow through them

a network of canals   then lifts off toward the sky

purls below the docks   fills the empty swimming pools

flickers in the windows across the avenue

hovers   a shadow beneath our speeches

lives in the shadows under the parked cars

plugs the barrels of rifles   is the weight in a swung fist

rises off the water when you enter the tub

lies in bed with us   thins between us when we press together

is cradled by the shoes in the dead man's closet

holds the echo of his weight   lowers like fog

when the sirens choke back their warnings

curls inside the shell that refused to explode   coats it

in a field of poppies painted across the casing

inhabits the hanged man's feet   but not the squeaking rope

fills the phone lines even when they carry our voices

threads its capillaries up the empty gutters

down the obsolete coal chutes

cups the nose of the plane   but not the tail

is the ear we whisper our fears against

the ear like a boat they lie down in

gets scattered with the darkness by the rasp of a match

slides back in

VIII

       ] they finished draining
the canal today, and there's talk

of building an underground train.
Mother pretends not to notice

the papers—she eats her biscuits
like nothing is happening!

It will be just awful here, I think,
the City a jittering web

of bridges. All our parasols
will blacken with soot!

—But then I imagine
pouring through the canal

in the panoramic dark of a rail car,
part of the current, and Liss,

I can hardly wait for the future! [

POEM SLIPPED BETWEEN
TWO LINES BY VALLEJO

It will not be what is yet to come, but
that which came and already left,

this abandoned pool—the water
now dust—the yellow light

in a window one notices
only when it goes out. The voice

of a gunshot, an unraveling
contrail. The widower's remove,

like virga. Each time
I step through myself, I land

in the next step that steps
through me again. When I lay

in the thickness of late summer,
listening to the news

on the radio, I caught each word
as it fell, because it fell.

———

In the empty diving well
the ladders are impossibly high,

and a world that isn't mine drifts
around and above me; light

once marbled by water lands
flat and vacant on the powder-

blue floor. Cesar, you ask
that I imagine your cell: motes

circling above you like bodies
husked by their movements

as you stir them. And later,
at your desk: nudging around

the intractable letters. I, too,
floated above you, here

———

in your unlived future: the deck
littered with tiles, the windows—

their browned light breaking
across the mute gutters.

Around me, the City is a bloom
of light in the nation's night-

black veil,—this jumbled
nation that never was yours.

Again, your words arrive
for me to fill silently

with my voice—not the voice
I'm speaking with now,

but that which came and already left.

NOTHING IN THE LETTERS: AN ELEGY

1.

Nothing in the letters
of the City outside his window,
the bells ringing at noon,

the sunlight a pale square
that crossed the bed then dropped

to the floor, the rasp of traffic
lifting through the wind, the cars
sliding underneath. Each day,

the sky dragged its light
through the surface of the river.

2.

In the rooms of his building
people drifted in and out

of themselves, as he had done
all his life, but then,
since he was dying, the City

closed down around him—
to that last room
with its dresser and sill,

the birdsongs joined to the space,
the clock knuckling forward,

the books with their words
all sealed up. There was nothing

left of the City but the hollow
of his dying. The window
was a painting.

3.

The words inside the books
belonged to the City—the words
he'd filled himself with,

that named the world
that was himself. The words
that, in dying, he gave back

to the City like sparks to the air—
no breath to hold them in

or push them out, just cells
rising among cells.

4.

But here: the tip of his mind
having rubbed its color
across the page, the pressure

his hand exerted—heavier,
then lighter—the black ink

lining this shallow canal
that loops, turns back
on itself, stops

sometimes mid-flourish.
Like the path of a leaf
gusting along a sidewalk—

5.

sealed like smoke
in a neon tube. (I can imagine

the smoke stirring,
some wind

moving through that space
inside the script.)

REPORT FROM THE DYING DISTRICT

At night, the bars are quiet. They cup light instead of music.

———

I scythe my boot against the weeds pushing stiffly from the curb.

———

The boulevard's pergola has been pulled down

by the vines it was meant to hold aloft.

(I once saw in that tangle two half-dressed homeless, fucking.)

———

The freight train passing at its requisite hour
is an empty trope sliding on the line of its sound.

———

I love the low rent and the artists who linger.

Their parties have the fervor
of those that occur in the middle of an occupation.

———

The houses one by one abandoning, each as if a wave has rushed inside.

Withdrawing, it leaves a trail of possessions in the yard.

———

I can track the movements of the only tenant in the complex up the street.

Her rooms turn on and off like footsteps

planting against the glass, then lifting.

IX

The gunbarrel chimneys
began to rise, and factory barracks

suited travelers just as well
as their worn-out saddles. Artists

were discovering abstraction—
which the City held in its promise

of geometry and vice as a camera
holds a world in its lens. The bars

were full of revolution—ideas!—belief
in Man since he made this context

from paper and sand. In the parks,
fireflies burned and flickered

like cigarettes on the balconies,
like the eyes of newcomers to the red-

light district. Each winter, snow
stripped the City of color—dusted

away the details—and the painters
loved this and tried to capture it.

Streetlamps hung their blown-glass
light down into the walks,

and lovers lingered to be seen
together in the glow. And when

fire spread from the newspapers
lying on the stoops, alley-piled

for the shopkeepers to start
their ovens, the City's light grew.

The shacks surrounding the market
burst their windows, and Sister

Meg's brothel lit the main square.
Those snowdrifts the painters

had loved were gone—but all
the next year, they painted fire.

THOSE BOYS

standing over the open grave
full of rainwater, looking down into it—

into their bodies, their soccer jerseys
thinned to smears on the surface,

the clouds drifting behind them
and through the grave beneath

where they're floating. A grave
they stumbled upon as they shortcut

through the field; the grave is empty,
they're pretty sure—abandoned

when the storm swept in so suddenly?
Each pictures himself as he was

when he heard the rain on the roof,
when the men must have grabbed

their shovels and trudged—to a truck?
Who was this grave dug for,

and where is he now? Those boys
want to know, gazing down

into the grave's turbid water,
a seedpod pressed to the surface,

a blade of grass—. Now a jet
slides in, etching its way;

one boy points down at it,
then another points too. What

do these boys want from this moment,
lingering above an open grave

full of rainwater? What will they say,
and to whom back home;

and how will it be explained?—
their reflections held

so precisely in the windless field—

THE WALL

All those years in the dark with our rattling spraycans

scrawling out curses at that half of the City

erased on the opposite side—.

As if they could read our words through the concrete,

as if what we wrote was for them, not for us.

Soon the wall was a thick net of language—

a false horizon—it built toward us

in minute layers that shifted

as we shifted, it mirrored the flashing of our voices.

On the other side, they, too, were writing us,

and then it was unclear what we should hate more—

those who were sealing us up in their dialect,

or the tangle we'd made

that had come to replace them. In the night

we could hear the hiss of their paintcans,

their sloshing buckets, and we tried to imagine

the words those noises conveyed. Who were we

but our language kissing theirs through the wall?

Who were they but the language we met

in the night for a kiss?

So that now, since the wall no longer exists

and each of us has a piece preserved on his desk,

I must say I'm not sure if this *i*

came from our side or theirs—

which word it belonged to,

what thought it once held

like a roof at its capital.

A TREATISE ON POWER (IN 32 STROKES)

(1) Even a leaf presses its weight against the table.

——

(2) In fog, the brighter the lights, the worse the driver's blinded.

——

(3) How traffic makes way for the flashing ambulance,

(4) then jostles to ride the wake of its passage.

——

(5) How the dead keep writing us from down there . . .

——

(6) And they who lay down in the fields
    to be shot—who's cushioned by their ghosts? Now

——

(7) the fan in the window is turned by the wind;

(8) now it makes the wind.

——

(9) Let's burn the leaders in effigy;
    let's beg for their return.

(From what space is the wind so endlessly hollowed?)

_____

(10) Tonight, the street's voice is

            [*glass breaking*].

(11) Tonight, death will empty somebody's face.

_____

(12) In the abandoned government building,

        papers covered the floor like spent lottery tickets.

_____

(13) How quickly we erase ourselves—

(14) in favor of abstractions.

_____

(15) And yet, people can become so cramped
    pressed up inside their words—.

(16) (And when they recede into their silences, sometimes
the words remain.)

———

(17) Observe you father
bend to kiss the wealth on a bishop's finger.

———

(18) Beyond the fence, a police helicopter
pinned to the ground by its spotlight—

(19) and by whomever the spotlight is trained upon.

———

(20) We find we're not who we said we were.

(21) We ask: is this always the case?

———

(22) It's impossible to enter a lake without chaosing the surface,

(23) and thus, how close *yellowcake* comes to being
the most beautiful word in the English language.

———

(24) Note how a young man looks

                        at a gorgeous nun,

———

(25) watch as a finely dressed woman gets her luggage
stuck in a revolving door.

(26) There's no better time for the bellhops
to take their smoke break.

———

(27) Without power, we'd be stuck in this elevator.

(28) Without power, the world's submarines would sink silently
to the abyssal plain.

———

(29) Let's remember:

(30) every direction meets in the compass rose of a body.

———

(31) So listen to how the body cries out!—

———

(32) how the wind dashes in to steal the echo.

X

And then war. Even balloons
became weapons, as did bottles

and kites and those strange
new flying machines the academics

had mocked for their uselessness.
Tanks ripped away cornerstones

in the Gothic District, cinemas
showed footage of whatever

was happening outside. (Some
joked the screen had become

transparent.) Cannons turned
the boulevards into aimed barrels,

and occupiers slept in the homes
of those who killed them. Everyone

was there; indeed, one Philip fought
hand-to-hand through the Garden

of Statues and later bragged
in the bars of killing four boys

beneath the Arch of Liberty.
After, when the City was reclaimed

and alliances were the new language,
when photographs of the body-

fields were developed, many
had had enough and poured out

into the country. They sowed
the land with long rows of houses

and cul-de-sacs pooled with rain.
But those who stayed found

they loved the City for its details
more than for its Grand Design

(their friends' deaths had been details
defending the Grand Design)—

plus: each of us remembered
the last-ditch plan to destroy it.

IN THE BARRACKS: A FOUND POEM

They had been in town only for a few days when the hills began pricking into the barracks (which once had been university classrooms) with sniper fire. That night, they crawled to their bedrolls in the corners, the cold spilling through the rooms like silt. There were no sandbags, and the bullets kept arriving,

solitary and oddly quiet—splintering the floorboards, cracking the lintel, the heavy door, tapping around in the billowing dark for just a second—to catch somewhere and the room went dull.

At dawn, four of the men crossed the courtyard to the library; when they returned they were pushing carts of books. In an act of uncertain desperation, they stacked them as high as they could in the windows, and that night the bullets came smacking into paper,

where they stuck. In the morning, Knox took down one heavy blue book and opened it: a bullet, surprisingly cold to the touch, had burrowed into the pages, which he lifted a few at a time from around the embedded snub—until it fell loose.

The shooter could not have intended to punch out the letters that were missing, Knox thought, yet they were gone. But the book could still more or less be read without them,

and he liked knowing that a bullet's approximate penetration through a treatise on the history of Western Europe was 350 pages.

BOMBING THE CITY

Some nights it was leaflets, others, incendiaries;

the citizens of the City waited patiently

for our issue. When our parachutes fluttered

pilotless to the ground, the people gathered

the silk to make stockings; when our duds

stuck in the plazas like darts, they collected them

to prop up their chairs. I was a bombardier;

I looked down the sight as if into the text

of a page. Later, beneath the canopy

of some distant truce, we dropped palettes

of food (which landed through skylights,

on street carts, on dogs—). And once,

when we opened the bays, all that came forth

was a silent billow of snow; it fell emptily

through the night. I imagined a flake

hitting the lens of somebody's glasses—

a fleck on his world. The rest they shoveled

into banks in the gutters. By noon it was gone.

XI

] I spent my childhood watching
the men repaint the chapel ceiling—

I imagined they were painting
the ceiling of civilization, imagined

their work would fill in the blue
above the roofline. [   ] I remember

chipped fire escapes, nests of wire
atop the electrical poles, clotheslines

tangled in the courtyard. [   ] Finally,
I was a grain of sand in a window.

And who was in the room behind me,
and what did they see through me? [

[THE CHILD'S CRY IS A LIGHT THAT COMES ON IN THE HOUSE]

The child's cry is a light that comes on in the house,
when the street is empty and the trees are still.
The light in the window gives voice to the cry,

so when the windows are closed, we still know
her voice is pushing against the walls of her room.
Her cry: a light that comes on in the house,

quivering the filaments in the bulbs, lifting
her parents out of their beds in the dark; at times
a neighbor's light will echo the cry. Her voice

arriving from what seems to be nowhere—
from inside such a tiny body, it comes on
and on, that cry somehow filling the whole house

when her parents are sleeping, when the world
is sleeping. Like a lighthouse beam it swings around
and out of her body, flooding the window, a cry

emerging from inside a dream, a need or fear
she can't yet utter; all there is is her breath
pushing the cry, the light coming on in the house—
and her voice: a light planted deep in the cry.

AFTER THE FEVER: A PASTORAL

After four months, the fever withdrew into her,

past the vanishing point, and now it was impossible

to remember how fully it had filled her,

like light soaking the tissue of a leaf. Outside,

the traffic thinned to a word—so we split a cigarette

on the porch with the speaker in the window

and listened to Robert Johnson press his voice

against the City (a crystal quivering in the microphone).

The heavy book in my hands never opened—

it was there only to keep me still.

When the last song ended, the notes dropped

from their thumbtacks back into the soil,

and then the sky had grown noticeably darker—

it wasn't late; it was simply going to rain.

XII

Then airplanes were the new
elevators. The frontier beyond

the walls became a park, and folks
went out to picnic and hand-feed

the animals. Who needed the old
myths to explain what was out there?

Still, the assassinations continued
as the motorcades slipped through

the barrios and court districts,
the garages and wrought-iron gates

to the countryside. Bombs kept
exploding in the subways, leaving bits

of the flags they were wrapped in.
And people missed the old myths:

they had little to tell their kids
before bed, when the futureless dark

came to scare them. So pictures
were pulled from the charnel houses,

held up to the flashbulbs for a kiss.
And this became *contemporary*: photos

propped beside people in motion,
people who ate popcorn and peanuts

at their tables, watched time shift
the stained glass in their screens.

THE RESCUE

All our debris above the sunken ship
                                —we among it—

in what seemed a chosen patch
                    of the sea's black gloss.

The pricked sky arced over like a slipcover; its edges

dipped into the water.
                    By the time the helicopters

dropped their spotlights and helibaskets,

white-rolled the surf
                    with the force of their hovering,

we lived only in the thought of our rising.

————

As we rose on our pallets of wire, I could see

the portholes far below, glowing
                    with those lights

we'd read by, dressed by, turned on and off blindly—.

Just beads now—clearly there,
                    but as distant from us

as a score is from its music. They dimly greened

the surface, pressed the debris
                              up into its meanings.

Then,
      just as we angled away, they all blinked out,

and the sea might as well have been empty.

ARCHEOLOGY

The twelve-tone scale
                still in its ancient box,

mud of sound
                washed from the pitches—

stars
        pulled from the sea's dark bottom:

arrange them in a line of fading constellations

and you have a song. Repeat the melody

until it lands in a music box's Braille. Or lie

back in the comet-tail
                        of your own paraph—

your formerly liquid line. Our papers

float on the water, intact
                        though tissue-delicate,

as our lives
        breathe us inside our clothes,

as our voices
        web the City Square,

push against each other across the tables.

And when the streets grow silent?—

listen to the ring
                 of an excavated bell,

upside down and full of earth.

XIII

Some kept burying the books
while others kept digging them up again.

CPR

Like striking a flint down into a basket of tinder—
a little damp, which spark will take?

———

And the live oaks arcing over the lot,
and the door that hasn't opened
                                    for a while, now,

the bouncer there in the narrow hall, the bass
heaving its waves against the inside wall.

———

The slim rush of a car passes
beyond the privacy fence, then

nothing else. The voicelessness of the work,
the ache in his back. And now

———

here's our fire: a man still breathing
his breath
            into a dead stranger's mouth.

OUR LAST VISIT

for my father

Streets opened onto streets,
doorways onto doorways. And there:

a courtyard of orange trees;
and there: the Ukrainian bar—
one stubbleface tipped forward

over his tumbler. So we passed
beneath the windows of deepset rooms,

their bookfilled interiors—that
honeyed library light. And farther,
steam rose from the sewer grates,

swelled from the candying peanuts,
the chestnuts fleshy and charred.

Linger before the tankers in the harbor,
the cavernous nostrils of horses;
I'll wade through the pool

of pigeons in the square, they'll rise
before me as though I were wind.

And the fan turning in the wall
behind the hotel, and the subways
riding forward together, their lights

joined in the tunnel—then sharply
veering away. We continued

down the steps, past pawn shops
and surplus stores; a man was sailing
tinfoil boats on a silent fountain.

Then the streets grew narrow,
thin terraces hung over us,—voices

like branches, like bowers of leaves.
A girl was selling spices in bags,
icons from a folded church.

Then a lovely face at a table—
we nodded hello—then a railing

and nothing but sea.

XIV

       ] and the cars on Grand
shifting raindrops from where

they'd aimed to fall. Porchlights
coming on, the theater

boarded and sealed shut
with the posters of exhausted shows.

The lot where last week a man
was stabbed hangs from its lights—

hangs like an empty sports field
sprouting weeds. And in the bars,

and in the shops, and in the market.
In the restaurants, the alleys,

the shadowy, overgrown courtyards.
Here's the cursor, and here's

my room inside it—. Tell me,
what words do we trail behind us?

Tell me, who slips them like chum
off the stern? Endlessly musing

the backstreets and boulevards,
cars crossing the faces

of shop mannequins. Then
the rain shifts to sleet

and the car tops to snares;
passers with their collars up.

A cab carrying its yellow
like a wind inside its motion;

a bare leg rising in a window.
A bare leg rising in a window . . .

—so at first I don't notice
the sleet has turned to snow,

but then the street is suddenly
quiet, as when a room

has been silenced by music. [

The Auden epigraph is from "Memorial for the City"; the Paz epigraph is from "I Speak of the City" (trans. Eliot Weinberger); the Calvino epigraph is from *Invisible Cities* (trans. William Weaver).

Throughout the book, many of the Roman numeraled poems were informed by Spiro Kostof's *The City Shaped: Urban Patterns and Meanings through History*.

"A Prayer (O City—)" (p. 3): William the Conqueror effectively won control of England in 1066 at the Battle of Hastings, where (at least as tradition has it) his opponent Harold II was hit through the eye by one of William's archers; Harold's men were then quickly routed. Whiteman Air Force Base, just up the road from where I teach, was the staging point for stealth bomber missions flown during the early period of the Iraq War. I've heard from people who work on the base that there's a particular Wal-Mart folding lounge chair which fits perfectly in the back of the bomber's cockpit for the pilot and mission commander to take turns napping in while crossing the Atlantic.

"Flooding the Valley" (p. 14): For example, the Tennessee Valley Authority constructed 16 dams between 1933 and 1944 and currently has more than 30 under its authority. Many thousands of people were displaced by the construction of these dams and their reservoirs. The electricity generated by the TVA allowed for rural electrification in the region, which private companies thought at the time to be economically untenable.

"III" (p. 19): During periods of plague in Europe, when a member of a household was found to be sick the house was sealed shut and marked with a cross, more or less condemning the rest of the family to death.

"A History of War" (p. 20) was partially inspired by Hew Strachan's *The First World War*, Kenneth Burke's concept of "logomachy," and the fact that societies tend to expand their vocabularies most rapidly in times of war. Mark 77 is the direct successor of Vietnam-era napalm and has been used in both Iraq and Afghanistan. Reportedly, soldiers in the field still refer to Mark 77 as "napalm."

"*I've Heard that Outside the City*" (p. 27): I imagine the poem's italics to be the equivalent of Socrates' covering his head when, in the *Phaedrus*, he presents an argument he's ashamed of.

"The Death of the Frontier" (p. 29): The Aristotle epigraph is from *Nicomachean Ethics* (trans. Ostwald Martini). The poem is indebted to Frederick Jackson Turner's "Frontier Thesis"—and to Professor Geoffrey Blodgett.

"Winter Pastoral" (p. 32): For Jeanne.

"V" (p. 34): The poem was partially inspired by Howard W. Haggard's *Devils, Drugs, and Doctors*. Thanks to Claire Hero, who loaned me the book (which, I'm sorry to say, I still have in my possession).

"The Assassination Lecture" (p. 35): A nod is owed to Murray Farish.

"The Beautiful City (in 32 Strokes)" (p. 37): I imagine these "strokes" to be brushstrokes.

"American Aubade" (p. 45): The Melville epigraph is from *Moby Dick*.

"American Nocturne" (p. 52): The Miller epigraph is from *Tropic of Cancer*. "Atopose" is a term coined by the Surrealist Group in Stockholm in the mid-1990s to describe a "non-place" in an urban environment—an "unused or abandoned interspace between different planned places." For more on atoposes, read Mattias Forshage's mini-essay: http://www.surrealcoconut.com/surrealist_documents/forshage.htm.

"VIII" (p. 62): For example, in Cincinnati, Ohio, in the early 20th century, the beginning of a subway system was built in the city's drained Miami & Erie Canal bed; a street—Central Parkway—was then constructed overtop the tunnels. The Great Depression hit just as tracks were beginning to be laid, and the project was halted; it remains unfinished to this day.

"Poem Slipped between Two Lines by Vallejo" (p. 63): Vallejo's *Trilce* (section XXXIII; trans. Clayton Eshleman). The lines in Spanish are: "No será lo que aun no haya venido, sino / lo que ha llegado y ya se ha ido, / sino lo que ha llegado y ya se ha ido."

"Report from the Dying District" (p. 69) is indebted to Czeslaw Milosz's descriptions, in *Native Realm*, of parties thrown in Wilno during the Nazi and Soviet occupations of Poland.

"A Treatise on Power (in 32 Strokes)" (p. 77): I imagine these "strokes" to be the counted-off strokes of a paddling.

"In the Barracks: A Found Poem" (p. 84): Nearly all the poem's narrative details are lifted from "Premature Anti-Fascist," an essay by Bernard Knox recounting his time in the Abraham Lincoln Brigade during the Spanish Civil War. The essay is from the Abraham Lincoln Brigade Archives and can be read at http://www.english.illinois.edu/maps/scw/knox.htm.

"Our Last Visit": (p. 98): My father, Wayne C. Miller (1939-2008).

ACKNOWLEDGMENTS

My thanks to the editors of the following publications, which previously printed many of these poems, sometimes in earlier versions (and/or with different titles): *The Antioch Review, Barn Owl Review, The Butcher Shop, Center, The Cincinnati Review, Colorado Review, Conduit, Copper Nickel, Crazyhorse, descant, FIELD, Green Mountains Review, Indiana Review, The Kansas City Star, The Laurel Review, Luna, Ninth Letter, Notre Dame Review, A Public Space, Quarterly West, Redivider, Shenandoah, Subtropics, The Tampa Review,* and *Witness.*

A number of these poems were published as a limited-edition chapbook, titled *O City*, by Cinematheque Press. Thanks to Nate Slawson for his dedication, generosity, and fine work.

"A Prayer (O City—)" received the 2009 Lucille Medwick Memorial Award from the Poetry Society of America; thanks to Elizabeth Alexander, Maury Medwick, and the PSA. "[The child's cry is a light that comes on in the house]" received the 2008 Lyric Poetry Award from the Poetry Society of America; thanks to Elizabeth Macklin and the PSA. "The Assassination Lecture," "The Dead Moor Speaks," "Dear Auden," "Identifying the Body" and "Archeology" received the 2007 George Bogin Memorial Award from the Poetry Society of America; thanks to Eleni Sikelianos, "the family and friends of George Bogin," and the PSA. "American Nocturne" received the 2007 Lucille Medwick Memorial Award from the Poetry Society of America; thanks to Tracy K. Smith, Maury Medwick, and the PSA.

Thanks to the extraordinary people at Milkweed—especially my editor, Daniel Slager. Also, Ethan Rutherford, and, retroactively,

Jessica Deutsch. Not to forget Kate Strickland. And, of course, Ben Barnhart and Patrick Thomas, purveyors of Manhattans.

Thanks to Joy Katz for her brilliant line edits.

Thanks to those who encouraged this book, read portions of it in manuscript, and/or whose conversations, insights, and support were invaluable along the way: Kevin Prufer, Joshua Kryah, Brian Barker, Eric Williamson, Whitney Terrell, Murray Farish, Claire Hero, Randall Mann, Sean Hill, D. A. Powell, Jim Cihlar, John Gallaher, Alex Lemon, Marcus Myers, Dan Beachy-Quick, Nicky Beer, Martha Serpas, Audrey Colombe, Marc McKee, Beth Bingham, Keith Pandolfi, Matthew Eck, Michelle Boisseau, Debra Di Blasi, Sam Witt, Hadara Bar-Nadav, Ray Amorosi, Phyllis Moore, and others I fear I've forgotten.

Thanks to my mother, and also to Neill.

As always, Jeanne—my love.

WAYNE MILLER is the author of two previous poetry collections, *The Book of Props* (Milkweed, 2009) and *Only the Senses Sleep* (New Issues, 2006). He also translated Moikom Zeqo's *I Don't Believe in Ghosts* (BOA, 2007) and co-edited both *New European Poets* (Graywolf, 2008; with Kevin Prufer) and *Tamura Ryuichi: On the Life & Work of a 20th Century Master* (Pleiades Press, 2011; with Takako Lento). The recipient of six awards from the Poetry Society of America, the Bess Hokin Prize, and a Ruth Lilly Fellowship, Miller lives in Kansas City and teaches at the University of Central Missouri, where he edits *Pleiades* and Pleiades Press.

To order books or for more information, contact Milkweed at (800) 520-6455 or visit our Web site (www.milkweed.org).

What have you done to our ears to make us hear echoes?
By Arlene Kim

The Nine Senses
By Melissa Kwasny

Sharks in the Rivers
By Ada Limón

Fancy Beasts
By Alex Lemon

Seedlip and Sweet Apple
By Arra Lynn Ross

Music for Landing Planes By
By Éireann Lorsung

MILKWEED EDITIONS

Founded as a nonprofit organization in 1980, Milkweed Editions is an independent publisher. Our mission is to identify, nurture and publish transformative literature, and build an engaged community around it.

JOIN US

In addition to revenue generated by the sales of books we publish, Milkweed Editions depends on the generosity of institutions and individuals like you. In an increasingly consolidated and bottom-line-driven publishing world, your support allows us to select and publish books on the basis of their literary quality and transformative potential. Please visit our Web site (www.milkweed.org) or contact us at (800) 520-6455 to learn more.

Milkweed Editions, a nonprofit publisher, gratefully acknowledges sustaining support from Amazon.com; Emilie and Henry Buchwald; the Bush Foundation; the Patrick and Aimee Butler Foundation; Timothy and Tara Clark; the Dougherty Family Foundation; Friesens; the General Mills Foundation; John and Joanne Gordon; Ellen Grace; William and Jeanne Grandy; the Jerome Foundation; the Lerner Foundation; Sanders and Tasha Marvin; the McKnight Foundation; Mid-Continent Engineering; the Minnesota State Arts Board, through an appropriation by the Minnesota State Legislature and a grant from the National Endowment for the Arts; Kelly Morrison and John Willoughby; the National Endowment for the Arts; the Navarre Corporation; Ann and Doug Ness; Jörg and Angie Pierach; the Carl and Eloise Pohlad Family Foundation; the RBC Foundation USA; the Target Foundation; the Travelers Foundation; Moira and John Turner; and Edward and Jenny Wahl.

amazon.com Bush Foundation jerome foundation

THE McKNIGHT FOUNDATION

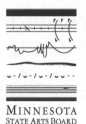

NATIONAL ENDOWMENT FOR THE ARTS
A great nation deserves great art.

TARGET.

MINNESOTA STATE ARTS BOARD

Interior design and typesetting by
Gretchen Achilles/Wavetrap Design
Typeset in Minion Pro
Printed on acid-free 100% post–consumer waste paper
by Friesens Corporation

ENVIRONMENTAL BENEFITS STATEMENT

Milkweed Editions saved the following resources by printing the pages of this book on chlorine free paper made with 100% post-consumer waste.

TREES	WATER	SOLID WASTE	GREENHOUSE GASES
7	**3,294**	**200**	**684**
FULLY GROWN	GALLONS	POUNDS	POUNDS

Environmental impact estimates were made using the Environmental Paper Network Paper Calculator. For more information visit www.papercalculator.org.